The Algebra of Inequality
& Other Poems
(2012-17)

Cliff Burns

Cover design: Chris Kent

Interior layout and design: Daria Lacy

Cover Art: "Where the Land Meets the Sea and Sky"
        by Cliff Burns

Published by Black Dog Press (blackdogpress@yahoo.ca)

Printed by: Lightning Source

Print edition: ISBN: 978-0-9938721-2-9
Ebook edition: ISBN: 978-0-9938721-3-6

BLACK DOG PRESS

"Myths are public dreams, dreams are private myths."
Joseph Campbell, *The Power of Myth*

"Terror seeks out the odd, and the sick, and the lost."
J.A. Baker, *The Peregrine*

With Regrets

I wasn't there at Srebrenica
so I couldn't block the bullets
or curse your executioners
as they cleansed you
out of existence

I wasn't in Kigali either
to seize all the machetes
scattering the mobs
with my shaming rhetoric

Never made it to Austria
to kill the little corporal
before he was born

etc. etc.

I've failed you at every turn
spading dirt over your
million separate faces
wiping my brow
before moving on to the
next field (and the next…)

plowed in deep furrows
hemmed with the dead

Sing *

"Sing her to light"
praise her in memory, your
mother   sister   daughter

Cherish her brief time
the way she smelled
when she was new

Call her "Angel"
for she has taken flight
left without a trace

*Written in response to "Walking With
Our Sisters", an art exhibition in memory
of missing and murdered Indigenous women

That Noir Moment

does it matter how far you fall
once you've fallen?
one small step or giant leap
a precipice or merely a pause

Munich, 1938

don't try appeasing me
like Hitler, I'll only demand more
of your ancestral territories
access to a warm, saltwater port

Chaos

history pretends unalloyed truth
its minions ascribing purpose
to consecutive horrors
vain order where there is none

Musing on Hawking Radiation, etc.

mathematics:
encroaching on God

provenance:
where we come from

expanding universe:
speeding toward dissolution

singularity:
all things are possible

Covenant

In our frailty
    grace
In our time of tribulation
    grace
In opposition to fear & despair
    grace
In the hour of our greatest need
    grace
In the midst of darkness
    grace
In our willing surrender
    grace
In spite of our pride & arrogance
    grace
In the knowledge that it is undeserved
    grace
In the name of all that is holy
    grace
In abject gratitude
    grace

Blameless

There is nothing sordid
about what we do.

For we act out of love.

Risk asperity, censure
for ignoring convention
so flagrantly.

Showing our defiance.

In tuneful harmony,
howling at the moon
under a shimmering borealis.

Oblivious of the neighbors.

How We Do It

you, brazenly,
as befitting a love
lacking all decorum
unabashed and erotic;

and me, playfully,
with slow, patient touch
because that is the way
you taught me

Camera Eye

I've left afterimages on your flesh
like spirit photography
indistinct outlines of our joining.

Enabling Mr. Hyde

I would not be afraid
except the last time this happened
the transformation was so complete
you did not recognize me.

Speechless

a typical paucity
as I try to produce the right sounds
communicate abject contrition while
simultaneously making my case for clemency

April

Winter subsides, withdraws/
receding and uncovering/
a shivering bareness/
raised gooseflesh, a slow blush/
spreading to every horizon

First Snow

Winter invariably defeats
the colorful palette
that precedes it

trees brutally denuded, stripped
of their plumage

hillsides and glens
made barren by the
mass killing of flowers

December flowers
glassine fragile
slow-dissolving
bright stains
marring the snow

Tribute

(for Sherron)

I'll write you a book
about two people
in a love affair
too improbable to be true.

Tell you a tall tale
boasting familiar faces
a couple that *might* be
me and you.

Shipwrecked

you are the tumult my life requires
out-witting dull routine, monkey-wrenching the works
keeping us ageless despite the slow accumulation of years
possessed by wonder, intimations of a higher power
concealed in the metronomic regularity
of the tides that stranded us here

Weak Moment

Tonight I think I'll be selfish,
refusing to disclose the shameful
extent of my passion, withholding
from you those sentiments I
normally share in this context
like a box of buttered popcorn,
except at the moment I find I'm
lonelier than usual, than I *should*
be, feeling the need to hoard
everything we are, keeping us
all to myself.

"the algebra of inequality" *

Once they enter the algorithms
consult their computer oracles
assigning dollar value to life & limb
with suitable aplomb

In the boardrooms of corporations
where the wolves run free
who will pay due compensation
for the sheep they slay?

* Title derived from "Report", by Donald Barthelme

Finity

(for Crad Kilodney)

"*Sic transit* something something"
like glory, memory fades

Don't let us be bashful:
I came, I'll stay awhile
and I shall die

The narcissist is dismayed,
the absolutist vindicated

"Back in 10 Minutes"

at the edge of the sky
where the clouds thin out
beyond the far horizon:
the evening star
hung on Heaven's door
like a notice left
by an absent shopkeeper

How Raven Kept His Name

Every day more animals
were brought before Adam
to be named and assigned
a place within the hierarchy
of living beasts

But many creatures resented
the presumption the ceremony
implied, "Raven" advising
the others to secretly retain
their ancient titles

Thus the descendants of Adam remain,
even now, mere shepherds, keepers
of domestic stock and fowl; no wild
thing will ever answer to its given name
or acknowledge our rightful dominion

Storm Season

Tonight, with the Perseics
ceaselessly returning;

In the light of a super moon
blazing in its hearth;

Under the firmament
pinholes in black velvet;

Another summer storm brewing
to further prevent the dark

September wind
chill, unsparing
rattling leaves
wilting whatever it touches

Autumn Palette

ochre   russet
    auburn   umber

yellow
    yellow-gold
        yellow-white...

that Adamic imperative
to *name*
    defeated by a glut of colors
    vibrant with disdain

Weather Report

night rain
invisibly descending
a saturating chill
bespeaking November

Nostalgic
(for Liam & Sam)

that bench
in the park
next to the
library where
we used to sit
tarrying awhile
on our way home
because it was
so warm, the day
so beautiful
and there was
      time to

unlike now,
hurrying past
some new errand
preoccupying me
hardly sparing
a sideways
glance at
our former
stopping place
the three of us
not so long ago
right over there
      remember?

Ghost

(Hodie mihi, cras tibi) *

barely inhabiting myself
in rooms nearly
as empty as I am

long, narrow doorways
always leading inward
futile circuits

endlessly repeated

* *"Today my fate, tomorrow yours."*

After the Robbery

My fence keeps me safe
Yours keeps me out

His fence is broken
Hers like a fortress

Some build a barrier of guns
Others leave a gate

Theirs is but a daisy chain
(God preserve their trusting souls)

Modern Music for Beginners

those Penderecki shrieks
sawing violins rhapsodizing
the fall of Berlin and
the depravities unleashed

Hiroshima shadows
courtesy the boys in the *Enola Gay*...

no wonder the atonality,
discord, when there were
places inside Auschwitz
no mere melody can describe

Insomniac

terror
abrupt/disorienting
like that dreaded midnight call
confirming what you already knew

nowhere
a harbor or sheltering cove
to deflect the tempest
absorbing the hours like blows

Sciatica

You can never call Pain *friend*.
It is quarrelsome, insistent,
practically inescapable
like a boorish relative one must
endure at weddings
and family functions
or a childhood pal,
now out-grown,
who always overstays their welcome.

Milky Way

They stopped counting at four hundred *billion*.
Just threw in the towel.
Resorted to a shorthand of equations, accompanied
by hair-pulling and other frantic gesticulations.

That's a lot of stars, of suns,
but still only one, single galaxy,
not an especially distinguished
galaxy at that.

Kind of humbling, isn't it?
To realize from a cosmic perspective we're
the equivalent of country bumpkins, living
wayyyy out in the boonies.

And so can any god suffice?
Persuade us of a divine flame
burning invisibly within us, shining
like one of those stars?

Or have you murdered faith,
Galileo, by measuring the glory of
Creation with your heretical gaze,
recanting except in your heart?

Desolate Angel

Let me be your dark side
that little voice insisting
all you think and say and do is
wrong
inadequate
mediocre
derivative

A constant, niggling reminder
that you aren't making a difference

When you're happy, I'll conjure overcast skies
when speaking of love, grant your face a leering cast
(and, anyway, you *know* it never lasts)

Alert for the merest glimmer
keeping vigil as you sleep
weightless, softly breathing
vivid dreaming your despair

Ticonderoga

Thick barreled befitting small clumsy fingers
grimly shaping consecutive rows of letters
extra marks for staying between the lines

bent studious anticipating a lifetime
toiling under shrill supervisors
documenting every shortcoming
critical of the slightest fault

laboring with little hope of reward
succeeding without getting ahead
ancient before their time

Harbingers

In our rush toward willful extinction
with the precipice clearly in sight
there you are, picking daisies
the fields & forests ablaze

You, who like to plead ignorance
or beg off, pressed for time—
explaining to your grandchildren
why they must suffer & starve

Song for You

If I shouted your praises
this morning
climbed King's Hill and
through cupped hands
serenaded the painted valley
with my *corrido* of longing
would you hear it
where you are
a whisper, a susurrus
pitched beyond sound yet
strangely pleasing to your ears?

14/02/2016

Forever isn't nearly long enough

No amount of time
allows for a passion
that defies the ages:
whole eternities contained
within the breadth of a kiss

Happier Days

when the overcast refuses
to yield the stars,
brighten the sky
with vivid recall:
that July night
in Prince Albert
when we stayed out
late for the Northern
Lights and were
rewarded with a
cosmos all to ourselves

Relativity

When we were young we
killed time indiscriminately
savagely using swords and
laser beams slaughtering it
by the hour with hyper-active
games mindless babble or just
lying on our backs drawing
shapes out of obliging clouds

Now time flees from us while
we are sleeping or otherwise
occupied each new morning
revealing the extent of the
damage and no matter how often
how hard we try to save or slow
time it runs down runs out always
too soon never long enough

The Taxonomy of Passing Faces

None of them seems capable of it.
They all appear so innocent.
Smiling, engaged in conversation.
You'd never suspect them of wrongdoing.
The terrorist they conceal within.

Today's Forecast

Autumn winds
presaging November
A weather system
originating in the
western Arctic
Rain, intermittent sleet...
Satellite images confirm
the worst still to come

Soundtrack

Ligeti is perfect for a
cold late autumn day in
Saskatchewan the first
flakes of snow visible
outside my window
trees audibly creaking
a stiff north wind
oblivious of the
bad news it bears

Strange Love

Stanley Kubrick's eyes belie dispassion:
remoteness was his only defense.
Look how frankly he regards you,
the way you shrink from that gaze.

Gallery

Normal is an absence of color.
Anger registers as red, blue
what happens when you
act on it.
White represents existence (so-called),
black the spaces between.
Orange when no other shade will do,
green & purple strictly prohibited.

A limited palette,
smears & blotches
where the paint has run,
a gaudy, priceless mess.

Philanthropy

I can't be miserly,
not with you—
loving you
requires largesse,
a generosity of
spirit, spending
kisses like pennies,
divesting myself
of a fortune in
the course of one
memorable night

Lucky Streak

Something like happiness
The resemblance uncanny.
Barely remembered, a phantom limb.
Missing fingers, invisibly crossed.

Faust

no deal:
your terms
too strict
your demands
too steep
the return
too small
my soul
too precious

De Civitate Dei

An Eternal City has
seven hills and a
creation myth.

It believes itself
descended from gods.

Even in decline it
retains imperial ambitions.

Omphalos: the center of the world.

Laying claim to its former
glory, while tourists take
selfies in the ruins.

Blue Bear Café

(Athens, Greece)

The pigeons
of Exarchia
are consummate
socialists—
surviving on crumbs
flocking communally
multi-colored
non-hierarchical
persistent as flies

Lord Elgin was a grave-robber

here
even the stones gleam
the fierce glare
of the Attic sun
scouring the ground
for its stolen riches

Aegean

blue-eyed vixen
coaxing us from safe harbors
mystified by our timidity

Kiveri

Paradise smells like fresh basil
frames like a postcard
tastes like fries cooked in olive oil
feels like a cool breeze on a hot day
sounds like rolling waves
tolerates stray cats and under-employed writers
leaves its mark like a saltwater kiss.

Analogy

Capitalism eats its sons and daughters
a cruel Thyristian feast—
dining in a palace of splendor
golden platters heaped with bones.

Varnavas

I am here
Lord
find me
on my
lofty perch
do not
deny me
your presence
forgive me
if I err
catch me
if I fall.

Cat Man

The stray cats of Istiklal Street
and the old man who tends them
though they be one-eyed
feral skinny
shying from our touch
collectively scowling
when we try to take their picture.

Eternal Riddle *

The "dawn visitors"
people disappeared
"behind the sun"
iron hands gripping
soft throats
freedom strangled
in its writhing womb
tell me, Pharaoh,
how many offerings you require
for your monument of sand?

* *Remembering Ozymandias, Nasser,*
Hussein, Assad & other Middle Eastern
potentates

Lineage

The cats of Istanbul
descended from Byzantine forebears
swift cagy cruel
territorial as Ottoman *beys*

Shipwatching on the Bosphorus

diesel-powered monstrosities
jockeying for position
upbraiding one another
with throaty shouts
only maritime etiquette
preventing disaster

captains of antiquity warned
against attempting these
treacherous Scyllian waters
the narrow strait & diabolical currents
inspiring tales of long, reaching arms,
an inescapable crushing grip

Strumpet

Prague, you old whore
coquette of *Mitteleuropa*
adorned in gothic finery
enduring the rough pleasure
of marauding hordes
secretly derisive of their
admiring gazes
offering your best
most familiar features
while assuring each of them
you've never done this before.

Meditation 1

(at Spaleny Mlyn)

A tree
at rest
motionless, yet
silently growing.

A stream
never ceasing
peaceful, yet
invisibly eroding.

Meditation 2

(Spaleny Mlyn)

Better to be a
slow-falling leaf
than a stone god;
to have lived,
however briefly,
not unremembered,
forsaken.

Heedless

the disregard of constellations
magnified by our clever mirrors;
the sky reaches up
but into nothingness subsides

Dark Matter

Space is mostly just that
nothing to commend an emptiness
that out-paces Time
spreading to inexorable dissolution

The Extinction Machine

born hungry
seeking a nipple
needful from their first breath

so delicate
requiring furs and hides
and, later, moisturizers and lotions

avaricious
hoarding and protecting unearned riches
the fruits of exploitation and privilege

in summation:
an immature species
quarrelsome and self-destructive

gift them with invention
technological marvels
knowledge beyond their ken

feed them the future
until they choke
on its fumes

Learned Behavior

we emulate our gods
by turns jealous and paranoid
desirous of silver and gold
hiding our indifference
behind impassive masks
reluctantly doling out favors
callow, prone to deceit

Nothing to do with rockets

hopeless trajectory
miles off course
navigational malfunction
spiraling out of control
threatening civilian populations
programmed for self-destruction
to prevent serious harm

Relativity (II)

Tomorrow feels like
yesterday
only newer.

Today is a fresh
coat of paint.

The past is right
behind the present
but losing ground fast.

Weep for the future:
child of our sins
waiting to be born.

Phobic

Never far away,
always lurking.
Brother Anxiety, Sister Fear,
playmates since childhood.

See World

window people
framed for a moment
like aquarium fish
exotically drifting

23/05/2017

The morning after the Manchester bombing
an old grey tomcat sleeps under a white maple
in our backyard, oblivious of human affairs,
indifferent to the harm we inflict on one another.

I wish I had his equanimity, then I wouldn't feel
so bewildered by a universe that seems to condone
random violence, so disappointed in a species that has
forgotten the simple joy of napping beneath a shady tree.

Night Letters *

anonymously posted
your notice of eviction
signed in blood

left on the threshold or
slid beneath the door
while no one is watching

some midnight hour
they will come
seeking your reply

gather what you can
slip out the back way so
the neighbors don't see

under cover of darkness
risking all you have just to
live one more day

* Referring to messages received by
suspected ISIS loyalists in Mosul,
Iraq, warning them of the reprisals
they will soon face from government
forces & their allies

Things that were lost in the flood

old photo albums a wedding
dress letters cards dating back
decades books so many books
bloated with moisture leaking
words a mush of ink plus the
kids' baby clothes mementos
curios keepsakes priceless to
everyone but the insurance
company which refuses to
process our claim denying
compensation for drowned
treasures a veritable fortune
in gold-encrusted memories
jewels baubles of bygone days

Eden

Versailles never looked
more beautiful than the
morning the mob entered
its grounds They were
baying for blood but
brought up short by its
exotic environs opulent
baffling to malnourished
minds Many wandered the
manicured gardens for days
afterward enthralled by splendor
ragged exiles granted one last
glimpse of Paradise before
its gates closed forever

Religion, summarized

Might as well fear the clouds
or prostrate yourself
before a 1000-year old
yew tree

Jesus, put away your cross
Mohammed, Buddha, no thanks

I'll practice my faith
in some special place
worship where there
are no altars

Golgotha

If there *is* a God, that
Supreme Being would
have to endure every
unkindness, every injury,
the abuse and mistreatment
of innocents, the unspeakable
acts we inflict on each
other, pain and torment from
time immemorial.

God would bleed and die
and scream and whimper
and *plead* for one more
breath of life, while expert
torturers worked their wiles,
wringing false confessions,
betrayals, a crown of thorns
carefully arranged just prior
to execution.

Liz Lake (Meditation)

placid
like water becalmed
no violent tide
tugging us from shore;
safe, at harbor
anchored against harm

In the Pink

The winter light is failing
color slowly draining from
a parched cold land
       Except a peachy glow
       seeping along the horizon
       cloud-tinged
       soft as old skin

Boreas*

your return imminent
the earth ritually donning
its splendid coat of fall colors

children once more confined
to their seats straight-backed
feigning docility

smoky skies from forest
fires in the west emit an eerie
orange light

as we prepare ourselves for
wintersleep blanketed by
a smother of snow

* Boreas: Greek god of the north wind

Meteorology

The weather these days is strange
overcast with a chance of melancholy;
on the weekend, the sun never shines
and the grass smells of tears.

Filling the Hole

"A bird's death leaves a hole in the sky."
Zbigniew Herbert

Shall I cling to the
hope that your
absence will be
made bearable
by memory?

Is it possible to
draw comfort
from old pictures,
keepsakes, things
that remind me
of you?

How long is forever
and will you have
the patience to wait?

Foreshadowing

It's getting darker
the storm approaching
preceded by distant thunder
a rising wind parting
the curtain for the
feature attraction.

When it arrives (and it will)
nothing can prepare you
for the ferocity, a force
that belittles prayer,
rattling and shaking
your leaking windows
making the children cry.

Default

There's less of me
        than there was before

I'm running down
        can't keep pace with Time

Days are shorter
        nights exponentially longer

Thinner, grey-skinned and sallow
        a sadness behind my eyes

People no longer speak deferentially
        all at once, I am a child

The future an unpleasing prospect
        find my refuge in the past

Grief

I'll take you out and look at you
one day, but for now I think I'll keep
you in a locked drawer, secured against
my curiosity, in the certain knowledge
there is no statute of limitations on *pain*,
while selfishly, vainly aspiring to somehow,
almost inadvertently, lose that precious key.

Contrast

The weather here is beautiful
even though you are dying.
Each day sunny and glorious
no acknowledgement of your suffering.
I draw a grateful breath
as you anticipate your last.
Looking forward to another dawn
while you confront endless night.

Definition

Grief: a fruitless yearning
for what has been lost.
Something irreplaceable,
the only key to a
lock that can no
longer be opened.

Anatomy

can hand erase the bruises it makes?
will mouth regret those hasty words?
do feet disobey the imperative of flight?
does heart have the capacity to forgive?

Passengers

We are poor
stretched beyond our means

We are young, old
a variety of colors

We are patient
(it's a long ride)

The bus is full
passengers squeezed side by side

Sol

Bees love yellow flowers
because they remind them
of the sun.

In the autumn
exploding supernovas
scatter petals to the wind.

Wildfires

distant fires darken
our skies

confused plants
shrivel in the
unexpected dusk

Black and White

magpies loudly proselytize
their pagan faith
provoking religious wars
with other creatures
who resent their
clamorous certainty

Assigned Reading

As Hazlitt once said
or possibly it was Spengler...
Plato thought of it first
or perhaps it was Aristotle
(I always get them mixed up)

The Greeks invented it
Anglo Saxons stole it
and the New World paid the price

Adam Smith put it best:
"Something something something something"
(though that's often taken out of context);
Hegel couldn't make sense of it
and, anyway, nobody tells it like Marx

Shooting the Messenger

Accused of preaching apocalypse
a latter-day Chicken Little
frightening the children
with visions of fire and flood.

Cast into the wilderness
exiled from the *ummah*
watching from the desert
as their cities burn.

Severe Weather Advisory

A system of fast-moving clouds
high altitude winds speeding
them toward their destination

> *If it storms, will it rain?*
> *If it rains, will it pour?*
> *If it pours, will we drown?*
> *If we drown, will you mourn?*

When the heavens finally open
a torrential shedding of tears
overflows every ocean and sea

> *If it storms, will it rain?*
> *If it rains, will it pour?*
> *If it pours, will we drown?*
> *If we drown, will you mourn?*

Find yourself an Ararat
from the highest precipice
watch for a flicker of wings

> *If it storms, will it rain?*
> *If it rains, will it pour?*
> *If it pours, will we drown?*
> *If we drown, will you mourn?*

Delinquent

Offer us a stick
we'll sharpen it to a point.

Provide us with clear, running water
we'll build a dam.

Show us how to plant a garden
we'll raid our neighbors' plot.

Teach us to sing
we'll write anthems.

Make up a god
we'll supply the jealousy and hate.

Manifesto

distort the human
figure to the extent
that it reflects the
depths of our
iniquity

no horizons
discordant planes
scraped and blasted
by the sear gaze
of conscience

The Grief Path

single file
no speaking
eyes down
one step, then another
bare feet
sharp stones
deliberately placed
for maximum effect

Notes:

I rarely submit my poems for publication—the process is, frankly, demeaning and these days many magazines demand authors pay mandatory "reading fees", a policy to which I am adamantly opposed.

And so very little of my verse is published elsewhere, most of it appearing either on my blog or, very occasionally, posted on Facebook.

There were a couple of exceptions this time around: "Covenant" was published in *Snapdragon* 2.0 and "Things That Were Lost in the Flood" was posted on the web page of *Here Comes Everyone*.

A number of the poems in *The Algebra of Inequality* were written during a month-long trip to Europe in 2016. That summer my wife and I visited Greece, Turkey and the Czech Republic and, whenever I could, I'd either be scribbling madly in my travel journal or trying to capture the essence of a moment with a poem. "Varnavas", "Blue Bear Café", "Kiveri", "Cat Man", "Shipwatching on the Bosphorus" and numerous others are examples of the latter. I have a vivid memory of scrawling "Blue Bear Café" on location in Exarchia (a very cool suburb of Athens), trying not to disturb Sherron, who was lightly dozing on the other side of the table, taking advantage of the shade...

This collection was compiled over the past five years and accurately reflects the love, hope, disappointment and loss experienced during that interval.

Slowly the water fills
the shapes of feet which have vanished..."(Z. Herbert)

*

Special thanks to Sherron Burns, Liam Burns, Sam Burns, Laird Brittin, Colleen Burns, Gord Ames and a few select others (you know who you are). Family and friends who, for reasons of their own, continue to support and encourage a literary maverick like me. I couldn't keep doing it without you, folks, and look forward to the day when your endless kindness and patience will be rewarded, karmically or otherwise.

C.B.
March, 2018

About the Author

Cliff Burns is the author of twelve books, including *So Dark the Night*, *Righteous Blood* and *Sex & Other Acts of the Imagination*. He has been a professional writer for over thirty years, his work appearing in magazines and anthologies around the world. He lives in western Canada with his wife, Sherron, and several thousand books.